Born to Win

DAVID O. OYEDEPO

CONTENTS

THE MANDATE

The hour has come to liberate the world from all oppression of the devil, through the preaching of the world of faith and I am sending you to undertake this task.

FOUNDATION FOR VICTORY

I was teaching a series of seminars in January 1984, when the Lord first spoke to me very clearly on steps to victory. I went head-long into scriptures to ascertain the Bible basis for personal victory in every individual life situation. The truth revealed in this book is a product of those studies. I have consistently preached these things, and the results have been unmatchable. There are great testimonies of victories in every sphere of life for those who have listened, and have cared enough to apply them. The word works more than magic.

It is quite true that there are many problems, hardships and difficulties in life; but that is not the whole truth. There are problems, but there are solutions. All life problems have solutions. There are as many victories as there are problems. You can experience constant victories in all life situations by a simple application of the revealed word of God.

God has done everything possible for your victory. He does not intend you to be down today and up tomorrow, and vice-versa. He wants you up always. The truth is: you can be victorious always. If you know what God says about you, and you care enough to do it, your victory is certain. By this, the world is in your control.

For whatsoever is born of God overcometh the world: and this is the victory that overcometh the world, even our faith.

1 John 5:4

Your victory is closely tied to your faith. That is your foundation for victory. It is not faith in your ability, qualifications, or any mundane thing, but faith in the Lord Jesus Christ and on God's irrevocable word.

Recognize that you are born a winner and a victor by virtue of your birth and parentage. You are not expected to be defeated by anything. You are seated far above everything that is earthly. You are above defeat and failure.

It is my fervent believe that you will be translated into a different level of victory as you receive the word revealed in this book. It is written for you.

Be blessed.

THERE IS WAR!

The first thing you must understand is that you are engaged in a spiritual warfare. If you do not know this, you have no right to victory. There is need for a battle, fight or competition before there can be a winner and a loser, as a winner does not emerge from a no-duel situation. This knowledge is important for your victory.

It will be ridiculous for you to claim to be victorious over no one. When you talk of being a winner or victory, it means a battle was fought. There are many indications of this in the Bible.

It is sad to see many believers live and walk without a sense of war. They are at "ease", and that is why they are constantly down. If an enemy is fighting you, and you do not seem to know it, you make his victory certain and easy. But the Bible has given a clear understanding that the Christian life is a life of constant war. It is war in itself. We get clear indications about the fight from the Pauline epistles.

Now thanks be unto God, which always causeth us to triumph in Christ...

2 Corinthians 2:14

The fact that God causes us to triumph means there is something to triumph over. You do not triumph over an easy situation. A triumph comes after a period of hard fighting, and when one of the contenders eventually emerges victorious.

You must know that you are engaged in a fight. In another place Paul said we are in a wrestling contest. We are not playing around. The fight is not one-sided. It takes two to fight. Whether you are ready to fight or not, the fight is on.

The devil has really sought to put the Church on the defensive. He is constantly putting situations and circumstances against the people of God. He wants you to be beaten all the time, but God wants you up and victorious always. That is why this is a fight.

For we wrestle not against flesh and blood, but against principalities, against powers, against the rulers of the darkness of this world, against

12

 *spiritual wickedness in high places.*

Wherefore take unto you the whole armour of God, that ye may be able to withstand in the evil day, and having done all, to stand.

Ephesians 6:12-13

You will never need an armour in a peaceful setting. It borders on insanity for a man to be heavily dressed after the manner of the Roman soldiers – with helmet, shield, breastplate, and sword - ready for battle at a time everybody is celebrating. That person will need quick attention from his psychiatrist. But we are given the picture that we are doing something important.

We are engaged in some serious battle. This is repeated over and over again in the entire Bible. We are in a battle. You, in particular, are engaged in this war. The devil has aimed at destroying your life; but thank God we are in a war against the devil.

It is very important for you to know who your enemy is. The best military strategist would want to know some basic facts about the enemy he is fighting. He will want to know who the enemy is, what his purpose is, and what resources are available to him. That is, he wants to know the strength and or weakness of his opponent.

IDENTIFYING YOUR ENEMY

The common thing people think and say in today's world is that they are being troubled by some form of bad luck that was transferred to them by their ancestors. Some claim their only problem in life is the old woman (popularly known to be a witch) in their village. Others have some strange opinions and ideas about their situations. They always try to explain the sources of their problems.

But the Bible has made it clear and obvious that your enemy is the devil. Many people find it difficult to believe this. Their minds have been so programmed to believing that some people are responsible for their problems. The point is, the devil will want to keep you from identifying him as your enemy, because he knows that the moment you identify your enemy, the battle is almost as good as won. He keeps blinding people to this fact. But know assuredly that the devil is your adversary.

> *Be sober, be vigilant; because your adversary the devil, as a roaring lion, walketh about, seeking whom he may devour.*
>
> 1 Peter 5:8

The devil is your enemy, it is not the herbalist or the witch. Your enemy is the devil. He is the source of every fight you are fighting. It does not matter what fight it is. God is not your enemy. If you are born again, God is your Father. The devil is the enemy. He is your accuser before God. He has sworn that nothing will go well with you. This is where the fight is. He does not want to see you progress. He wants to ruin your business. He is always mounting pressure on you, to keep you away from God. He is not interested in any good thing coming your way. His thoughts towards you are completely evil.

Just as God is light, so is the devil darkness. Just as there is no darkness in God, so there is no light in the devil. He is complete and absolute darkness. This is the fight. He is determined against you. That is why Paul said, *"We wrestle..."*

It takes determination to wrestle. Nobody ever goes into the wrestling ring lightly. He must go with some ruthless determination to win. He must be victory-hungry to go into the ring, else he will be carried out unconscious. I want you to realize the level of hatred the devil has for you. He has no bit of love for you. He is your archenemy. He is wages war against you.

The battle you are engaged in is not physical. The devil is a spirit, so you cannot fight him physically. It is a spiritual battle that is fought spiritually. A physical problem has physical solutions and a spiritual problem can only be solved spiritually. If you look closely at Ephesians 6:12, you will notice a few remarkable things.

For we wrestle not against flesh and blood, but against principalities, against powers, against the rulers of the darkness of this world, against spiritual wickedness in high places.

Ephesians 6:12

It says we wrestle not against flesh and blood! Not human beings either. They are not your enemies. The devil has used this particular lie to disorganize and disintegrate homes and families. It is the devil at work. Notice that it says, *"…but against principalities, against powers, against the rulers of the darkness of this world, against spiritual wickedness in HIGH PLACES."*

These are not human beings. They are Satan's angelic authorities. They are sent by him to carry out his purposes and plans in your life. Stop looking at human beings as your problem. God has not called you into a physical fight, but to a fight of faith.

Please get hold of this truth. It will change your whole outlook, and you will be able to channel your spiritual energy in the right direction.

You may begin to wonder why God created such an

enemy to trouble you. The truth is that God did not create him a devil in the first place. God created him perfect in beauty. He had tremendous glory in heaven. In fact, he was the highest in the hierarchy of angels. The Bible describes him as the angel "that covereth"! He had the unique assignment of covering God's exalted throne.

> *Son of man, take up a lamentation upon the king of Tyrus, and say unto him, Thus saith the Lord GOD; Thou sealest up the sum, full of wisdom, and perfect in beauty.*
>
> *Thou hast been in Eden the garden of God; every precious stone was thy covering ... the workmanship of thy tabrets and of thy pipes was prepared in thee in the day that thou wast created.*
>
> *Thou art the anointed cherub that covereth; and I have set thee so: thou wast upon the holy mountain of God; thou hast walked up and down in the midst of the stones of fire.*
>
> *Thou wast perfect in thy ways from the day that thou wast created, till iniquity was found in thee.*
>
> Ezekiel 28:12-15

He was not created a devil. He was perfect in heaven, he took care of the throne of God. He walked before God; but became Satan when iniquity was found in him. As a result, he was cast out of heaven. It took violence to eject him. He was forced out and cast unto the earth. From that day, he made up his mind to fight against God. He is always pitching his tent against God and His people. That is why he is your enemy.

Check the scriptures. He has always been at variance with God's plan. He went into the garden, tempted Adam, and caused him to rebel against God. He corrupted the world till it became so evil that God had to destroy it (Genesis 6). He smote Job with sickness and caused all his belongings to perish. When Daniel prayed, he sent one of his fallen angels to withhold the result. He is traditionally anti-God, and has not left you out in this fight. He is constantly on duty to ensure that he does not lose the battle. If you look around you – the circumstances and situations around you – you will notice that this is true.

Look at the world today. Many terrible things are happening. New deadly diseases are being injected into the world by the devil. He wants to destroy God's crown of creation – man. Every evil in the world today is the devil's handiwork. God does not tempt any man with evil. He cannot destroy what He has created.

This fight can come in any way. It may be in the area of health. It could be in other areas like: need, spiritual growth, family problems, academic frustrations, in fact, in all areas of life. When these things come against you, recognize that it is the enemy, the devil, that is shooting his fiery darts at you.

The problems will come. Your own fight must come. You cannot escape it. Every believer is involved in it. You cannot say, "I am not fighting any battle." Your own battle must come, and you will fight it. My battles will come too, and you cannot fight them for me. I cannot fight yours either. Every individual will fight his battle.

When thou passest through the waters, I will be with thee; and through the rivers, they shall not over-flow thee: when thou walkest through the fire, thou shalt not be burned; neither shall the flame kindle upon thee.

Isaiah 43:2

This confirms that the time for you to pass through the waters and the rivers will come. He said, "When thou passest...", not "if." "If" makes it conditional, but "When" makes it certain. *That ye may be able to stand in the evil day...* (Ephesians 6:13).

The evil will come; you cannot dodge it. It is part of the things you will need to go through to get your victory. You cannot live in victory if there is no problem. If you do not go to war, you cannot bring laurels home. It is basic that hard times will come; but you know you can have your victory always.

One thing is certain about your fight. It is a decided issue. You are already a winner. God has done everything that is necessary for your victory. The devil has lost the battle. You are the winner. The problems will come because, *"many are the afflictions of the righteous...."* But you have been guaranteed victory already because *"... the Lord delivereth him out of them all."*

The devil is not the winner; you are! He is not a conqueror; you are more than a conqueror. Your lot with God is victory always. He causes you to triumph always on the basis of the finished work of Christ on the cross. That is your touchstone for victory. It was there that Jesus did it all.

The enemy's mission is three-fold. They form his ministry towards you. This ministry is clearly stated in John 10:10 by Jesus himself:

The thief cometh not, but for to steal, to kill, and to destroy...

John 10:10

The devil, your enemy, is the thief. He is not coming physically to break into your house or to snatch your car (he can do this, however, through his human agents), but he has ways of stealing your money, time, health, and even your property and he will do all he can to fulfill this ministry.

You have to know that each time you have a fight in any area, the devil is behind it. He is the unseen hand behind every evil thing. Any time you are attacked by sickness, it is an attempt of the devil to steal your health, joy and money, and even your life. The devil is desperate about this. He can throw anything at anybody, as his ultimate aim is to destroy. He is the enemy. If you know this, you will stop finding reasons and excuses for your problems, and you will be able to tackle them properly.

God is not the author of evil. He does not tempt anybody with evil. The devil is the master of evils. He is the source. Jesus said whenever he comes against you, it is to steal, kill and destroy. That is his plan. But Jesus also said:

> *...I am come that they (you) might have life, and that they (you) might have it more abundantly.*
>
> John 10:10

As the devil is totally committed to doing evil to

you, Jesus is absolutely eager to give you an overcoming life.

The enemy's evils cannot overpower the winning life Jesus has come to give to you. Jesus has given you that life – eternal life - by which you can win all the time.

There is no excuse for any believer to be defeated. God has perfected your victory programme in Christ Jesus. You can boast of constant victory. He causes you to triumph always over every situation. If it is sin, the Bible says he that is born of God does not sin. He has planted His seed in you, and you cannot sin if you abide in Him.

> *Whosoever abideth in him sinneth not: whosoever sinneth hath not seen him, neither known him.*
>
> *Whosoever is born of God doth not commit sin; for his seed remaineth in him: and he cannot sin, because he is born of God.*
>
> 1 John 3:6, 9

This talks about victory over sin. This is important, because the moment the devil can get you defeated in this area, you are finished. He can then go on and afflict you with anything and get away with it. The seed of God is in you. Eternal life has been planted in you. This life is stronger than any fight the enemy can bring. It is the very life of God that cannot fail in any situation.

Your victory is guaranteed in every sphere of life. Name it. God has provided victory for you in every battle in the comprehensive finished work of Christ at Calvary.

> *There hath no temptation taken you but such as is common to man: but God is faithful, who will not suffer you to be tempted above that ye are able; but will with the temptation also make a way to escape, that ye may be able to bear it.*
>
> 1 Corinthians 10:13

There is, clearly, no battle that is beyond you. If it was beyond you, God would not have allowed it to come your way. Do not think that God is unaware of your situation in battle. He knows your capacity as a winner. He knows what situations come your way. So before He allows any of them, He has assessed your strength. You have divine ability to win in all and every battle that comes your way. You are born of God, and whatsoever is born of God simply overcomes the world (1 John 5:4).

By virtue of your birth, you are a world overcomer. That is the Bible. The greater one is in you, and you are more than a conqueror.

The problems may look stern. The seas may rage, and the storm may be tempestuous, but in all these you are more than a conqueror. Every trouble seeks to separate you from the love of Christ; but the word says they cannot. They are not designed to draw you away. They are supposed to be stepping stones to victory. Each time you win a battle in faith, you are promoted. Your faith gets stronger; ready for another round. That is why the Bible says having done all, to stand.

> *Who shall separate us from the love of Christ? shall tribulation, or distress, or persecution, or famine, or nakedness, or peril, or sword?*
>
> *Nay, in all these things we are more than conquerors through him that loved us.*
>
> *For I am persuaded, that neither death, nor life, nor angels, nor principalities, nor powers, nor things present, nor things to come,*
>
> *Nor height, nor depth, nor any other creature, shall be able to separate us from the love of God, which is in Christ Jesus our Lord.*
>
> Romans 8:35, 37-39

This catalogue of things cannot separate you from the love of Christ. They cannot defeat you. Look at those issues again. They are the toughest battles you can ever fight, but they are not sufficient to defeat you. There is something too strong for the devil to break in you – the God-kind of life. This life was made available when Jesus died on the cross.

THE DRAMA AT CALVARY

The greatest event in the world's history was the drama at Calvary, when and where Jesus, the Son of the Most High, died. It was a time when the most unusual thing (both physically and spiritually) happened. The Creator of heaven and earth was crucified by His creatures It was the tragedy of all ages but much more, it was the deliverance and absolute emancipation of the world from the house of bondage.

In the book of the beginnings (Genesis) we are given the account of creation. God by sovereign act created the earth and formed His man, Adam, in His own image. He put him in the garden and made him the god of all His works. He asked him to reign, rule and exercise dominion over every living thing on earth. At the end of it all, Adam became the god of this world. God's plan in the beginning was perfect. Adam was to manage heaven's affairs here on earth. This happened, and everything went on smoothly. There was no personality clash between the God of heaven and the god of this earth. After all these, God looked and saw that it was very good.

> *And God saw every thing that he had made, and, behold, it was very good...*
>
> Genesis 1:31

Such was the beauty of God's work. He was satisfied with it. He said, "Very good!" With man at the helm of affairs, it was very good with God. He brought the animals to him for their naming ceremony. Adam gave them names, and God did not correct or change any of them till today. Such was the totality of man's dominion and authority. He did not need to struggle for victory, it was his habit. It was natural with him. He had God's very nature. He knew himself as the god of this world. It was easy for him to rule, because of his proper understanding of himself.

Satan, your enemy, did not enjoy this situation. So

he tempted God's man and got him to sin against God. Tragedy struck, and the devil took over the administration of this world. It was legally handed over to him by Adam, and no one could take it back except a man.

Immediately, man fell from his exalted state. He was literally "born again." He took upon him the nature of Satan. He became one with the devil in his satanic nature of spiritual death, and was thus separated from God. But God in His divine and predeterminate counsel had planned the drama at Calvary as the only way to retrieve the world, and to restore His man to his former estate. He then announced His plan publicly to the hearing of the devil that He, God, would send a Saviour that would defeat the devil.

> *And I will put enmity between thee and the woman, and between thy seed and her seed; it shall bruise thy head, and thou shalt bruise his heel.*
>
> Genesis 3:15

From this day, God set all His machinery into motion, and the devil began to wait and to expect with unprecedented anxiety. He started some hit and run strategies. He knew God to be true, that the counsel of the Lord shall stand for ever. He knew God's nature of constancy and consistency, so he began to panic. He caused so much problem in the world, that God got angry and destroyed it.

> *And God saw that the wickedness of man was great in the earth, and that every imagination of the thoughts of his heart was only evil continually.*

> *And it repented the LORD that he had made man on the earth, and it grieved him at his heart.*

> *And the LORD said, I will destroy man whom I have created from the face of the earth... for it repenteth me that I have made them.*
>
> Genesis 6:5-7

When God spoke those words, the devil must have been happy. If He destroyed the whole world where would the seed of the woman come from?

> *But Noah found grace in the eyes of the LORD.*
>
> Genesis 6:8

God kept His promise, and the Lord Jesus Christ came into the world.

Jesus came to give you victory. He did not need any miracle. He did not need to defeat Satan. He did not need to be saved. He is the Creator. He is God. He has been God from the beginning of the beginning. He is co-eternal with the Father.

He would not have needed any contact with the devil, if you were not involved. The devil is too inferior to Him for any conversation, talk less of a battle. Jesus Christ, He is the Lord! But He came, not as God. He came in the flesh, like a man. He was constantly referred to as the Son of man.

Understand that Adam legally sold out to the devil. He submitted to him as a man. So, it would take a man to take it back. God could have slapped the devil out of existence the moment man fell, but He did not. The devil would have accused Him of injustice. God did not give him authority; it was given to man, and it would take a man to collect it back.

So Jesus came as it was prophesied, and the devil started pursuing Him all over the place. It started from His birth till the time He died on the cross. Jesus came as a man.

Forasmuch then as the children are partakers of flesh and blood, he also himself likewise took part of the same; that through death he might destroy him that had the power of death, that is, the devil;

For verily he took not on him the nature of angels; but he took on him the seed of Abraham.

Wherefore in all things it behoved him to be made like unto his brethren, that he might be a merciful and faithful high priest in things pertaining to God, to make reconciliation for the sins of the people.

Hebrews 2:14, 16-17

Jesus did not come in the nature of angels or in His nature as God. He came as the seed of the woman, the seed of Abraham. He was made like us (totally man) to be able to confront the devil legally. He humbled Himself to become a man.

Who, being in the form of God, thought it not robbery to be equal with God:

But made Himself of no reputation, and took upon him the form of a servant, and was made in the likeness of men.

And being found in fashion as a man, he humbled himself, and became obedient unto death, even the death of the cross.

Philippians 2:6-8

He emptied Himself and came as a man to the world. Many people believe that Jesus performed those miracles because He is the Son of God. They say, "You cannot compare yourself with Jesus." But Jesus did those things as a man anointed with the Holy Ghost. He did not perform any miracle until after the Holy Ghost had descended on Him.

How God anointed Jesus of Nazareth with the Holy Ghost and with power: who went about doing good, and healing all that were oppressed of the devil; for God was with him.

Acts 10:38

He did not get those victories as the Son of God, but as a man. Even if He did in His sonship capacity, you are also a son of God, a bonafide member of the cosmic family.

Jesus so manifested the Kingdom power and authority that it put the devil on the defensive constantly. He tried all he could to stop Him, but could not; so he planned and framed charges of mutiny against the Lord Jesus Christ, who finally had to go to the cross for the greatest drama in the history of the world.

The Lord Jesus knew what was happening. He was fulfilling prophecy. But the devil was ignorant. He thought he had got the Son of God finally. Jesus was bridging a gap between the past and the future. The cross became the centre of history. Jesus the Messiah was on the cross.

More things happened on the cross than most people know. As He hung on the cross, great things began to happen in the realm of the spirit. He took the place of man in sin, sickness, poverty, death, and

33

every evil thing in the world. He was God's sacrificial Lamb for man's redemption from the hands of the chief task master, the devil. Right there on the cross, He was made sin. He identified with man in the sin situation. He identified with man in his fallen state and became sin for us.

For he hath made him to be sin for us, who knew no sin; that we might be made the righteousness of God in him.

2 Corinthians 5:21

Jesus became sin. Until this time, He did not know sin. But for Him to deliver man from the power of spiritual death, He had to partake of it. As He hung on the cross, He was sin personified. All the sins of the world, past, present and future were laid on Him. He died spiritually – separated from God.

He did not only carry our sins on Him, He carried the whole world's diseases and sicknesses as well. He carried all pains and afflictions. Every evil thing in this world was laid on Him on the cross.

Surely he hath borne our griefs, and carried our sorrows: yet we did esteem him stricken, smitten of God, and afflicted.

But he was wounded for our transgressions, he was bruised for our iniquities: the chastisement of our

34

peace was upon him; and with his stripes we are healed.

Isaiah 53:4-5

These things were accomplished on the cross when He said, *"It is finished"* (John 19:30). That was when it happened. When Jesus said it, He gave up the ghost. He finished your battles against sin, difficulties and every evil.

People argue that Jesus did not die spiritually. They are fully persuaded that He only died physically. If He only died physically, then He redeemed us from physical death only. It did not affect sin. Sin is a spiritual force, which no physical exercise can stop. Jesus did more than die physically on the cross. He also died spiritually.

He was made sin. Not that He sinned ordinarily, but He was made sin itself. He was sin incarnate on the cross. That is spiritual death. What does it take to be in a state of spiritual death? Spiritual death means separation from God.

Adam and Eve did not die physically when they ate the fruit in the garden, yet God told them, *"The day that ye eat ye shall die."* They did not die physically, but spiritually, as they were separated from God.

Jesus too was separated from God. Right there on the tree when He had become sin, God turned His eyes from Him, and Jesus exclaimed, "Father, why have You left Me alone?"

> *And when the sixth hour was come, there was darkness over the whole land until the ninth hour.*
>
> *And at the ninth hour Jesus cried with a loud voice, saying, Eloi, Eloi, lama sabachthani? which is, being interpreted, My God, my God, why hast thou forsaken me?*
>
> Mark 15:33-34

His Son was separated from Him. He had been made sin, and God is too holy to behold sin. His eyes are too pure to look upon sin. He had no choice than to forsake His Son on the cross. Habakkuk 1:13 says:

> *Thou art of purer eyes than to behold evil, and canst not look on iniquity...*

So Jesus, being sin at this time, could not continue to command God's fellowship. That is the whole essence of spiritual death.

It is a basic spiritual law that if any man is found with sin at death, he must go to hell. *"The soul that sinneth it shall die."* At this time the enemy thought he had got all the victory. He had finally succeeded in killing the Hope of the world.

He was even more excited when he noticed sin on Him, because it became imperative that He should go to hell. God would not break that law, else the deliverance of the world would not be complete. It would have been aborted.

> *And he made his grave with the wicked, and with the rich in his death...*
>
> Isaiah 53:9

If Jesus did not go there, then we would still have had to go there, because it means that His sacrifice did not cover that area. But Jesus took part in every thing that mattered to our redemption.

> *Wherefore in all things it behoved him to be made like unto his brethren, that he might be a merciful and faithful high priest in things pertaining to God, to make reconciliation for the sins of the people.*
>
> Hebrews 2:17

That is the whole truth.

> *Now that he ascended, what is it but that he also descended first into the lower parts of the earth?*
>
> *He that descended is the same also that ascended up far above all heavens, that he might fill all things.*
>
> Ephesians 4:9-10

The man David, in one of his prophetic psalms

about the Messiah spoke of the Lord Jesus in conversation with the Father.

> *Therefore my heart is glad, and my glory rejoiceth: my flesh also shall rest in hope.*
>
> *For thou wilt not leave my soul in hell; neither wilt thou suffer thine Holy One to see corruption.*
>
> Psalm 16:9-10

When Peter preached his first open air crusade in Jerusalem on the day of Pentecost, after he had just received the baptism in the Holy Ghost, he said this psalm is talking about Jesus.

> *For David speaketh concerning him, I foresaw the Lord always before my face, for he is on my right hand, that I should not be moved:*
>
> *Therefore did my heart rejoice, and my tongue was glad; moreover also my flesh shall rest in hope:*
>
> *Because thou wilt not leave my soul in hell, neither wilt thou suffer thine Holy One to see corruption.*
>
> Acts 2:25-27

His presence there was part of the divine assignment. He went there and finished the work. It was there that He cemented the victory and sealed the devil's doom and defeat. He took the keys to hell and death, and arose victoriously. He spoilt, defeated and stripped principalities and powers of all their authority. Before

this time, the devil had the power (key) of death. But when Jesus died and went to hell, He destroyed the devil and the powers he had.

> *Forasmuch then as the children are partakers of flesh and blood, he also himself likewise took part of the same; that through death he might destroy him that had the power of death, that is, the devil.*
>
> Hebrews 2:14

> *And having spoiled principalities and powers, he made a shew of them openly, triumphing over them in it.*
>
> Colossians 2:15

This is the culmination of the drama at Calvary! Jesus did a very neat job. He finished everything as it was written of Him, and rose triumphantly! He went to the throne and offered His blood as the blood of eternal covenant, and sanctified us for victory forever more. This is the springboard for victory. The cross is the touchstone for our victorious living. It is what settled the sin problem.

He took you out of the house of bondage, and brought you into life. He gave you life through His victory on the cross. He restored you back as God's man on earth. Jesus restored everything that man had lost in the garden of Eden in His victory over

Satan. He has put them all back into your hand.

The victory is total – spirit, soul, and body. It is a comprehensive victory for you in all ways. He did it on your behalf.

CHAPTER 3

YOUR NEW STATUS

When Jesus died and rose from the dead, He went into the Holy of holies in heaven to present His blood of eternal redemption on the basis of His substitutionary death and resurrection on our behalf. By this He obtained eternal victory for us, and made us victors over the devil.

...But by his own blood he entered in once into the holy place, having obtained eternal redemption for us.

Hebrews 9:12

He offered His blood at the holy place for us. It was not the blood of bulls and goats, but His very blood. After doing this, He sat down at the right hand of Majesty on high, expecting His enemies to be made His footstool.

But this man, after he had offered one sacrifice for sins for ever, sat down on the right hand of God;

For by one offering he hath perfected for ever them that are sanctified. Hebrews 10:12, 14

When He sat down on the right hand of God, He had completed man's perfect victory in all battles of life, because in that exercise, man (you) was legally identified with Him in His crucifixion, death, burial, and resurrection.

If you are going to walk in your victory, you must be fully aware of your identification with Christ in every stage of His redemptive work. In every stage of it, you were in Christ. You were legally present there, defeating the devil when Jesus died. When you know this you will develop a victory mentality, you will be conscious and aware of your legal victory in all battles of life as they come.

Just as Jesus identified with us in our spiritual death, we also identified with Him in His sufferings. We legally took part in it. If He did not identify with us, He would not have been able to redeem us. If we were not identified with Him also, we cannot claim any right to victory. But thank God we were identified with Him in His crucifixion, burial, and resurrection.

That is our victory. Consider the following scriptures:

I am crucified with Christ: nevertheless I live...

Galatians 2:20

Knowing this, that our old man is crucified with him, that the body of sin might be destroyed, that henceforth we should not serve sin.

Romans 6:6

Who was delivered for our offences, and was raised again for our justification.

Romans 4:25

He was delivered up on account of your trespasses, and raised for your justification. He became identified with you on the cross, and you with Him. You were there on the cross crucified. Crucified with Him, you also died with Him. You were joined with Him in the likeness of His death. As He died, you died with Him. As a matter of fact, you went to hell with Him. Complete identification!

For if we have been planted together in the likeness of his death, we shall be also in the likeness of his resurrection.

Romans 6:5

You were buried with him in His death. Water

43

baptism is a kind of burial with Christ. It is a type of His burial and resurrection. We virtually, legally took part in everything that happened to Him.

> *Know ye not, that so many of us as were baptized into Jesus Christ were baptized into his death?*
>
> *Therefore we are buried with him by baptism into death...*
>
> Romans 6:3-4

You equally identified with him in His resurrection and exaltation. You were made alive with him.

> *And you, being dead in your sins and the uncircumcision of your flesh, hath he quickened together with him, having forgiven you all trespasses.*
>
> Colossians 2:13

> *Even when we were dead in sins, hath quickened us together with Christ...*
>
> Ephesians 2:5

When Jesus was made alive in the Spirit, you were also. On the basis of identification you were raised up from the dead together with Him.

> *And hath raised us up together, and made us sit together in heavenly places in Christ Jesus.*
>
> Ephesians 2:6

When God raised Him up and exalted Him far above

principalities and powers, you were there with Him – exalted. *"And hath raised us up together, and made us sit together in heavenly places in Christ Jesus."*

That is you! He raised you above your enemies; you are far above them. You are over them.

> *...When he raised him from the dead, and set him at his own right hand in the heavenly places,*
>
> *Far above all principality, and power, and might, and dominion, and every name that is named, not only in this world, but also in that which is to come:*
>
> *And hath put all things under his feet, and gave him to be the head over all things to the church,*
>
> *Which is his body, the fulness of him that filleth all in all.*
>
> Ephesians 1:20-23

In identification, you were raised together with Him far above all your enemies. He put them under His feet – your feet. He did it for the body – the Church. Now, every principality is under your feet. That is the secret of your victory.

Note that you are in God's class of being. By virtue of Christ's redemptive work, you have become a new creation, if you have accepted Him as Saviour and Lord of your life. This new status grants you entrance into

God's class. You become a new creation at new birth. Completely new. Brand new; not an adjustment. Not a modification of the old status. You have come into a new status of being.

> *Therefore if any man be in Christ, he is a new creature: old things are passed away; behold, all things are become new.*
>
> 2 Corinthians 5:17

By this new creation you have become accepted in the beloved, in the family of the Father God. You have become a member of the cosmic family. You are, therefore, translated into the kingdom of God at salvation.

God declares you righteous. He becomes your real Father, and you become His real son. He comes into you with all His strength, glory, and majesty, and makes you strong in Him. He took you out of the powers and kingdom of the devil and translated you into the kingdom of the Son of His love.

> *Who hath delivered us from the power of darkness, and hath translated us into the kingdom of his dear Son.*
>
> Colossians 1:13

In the kingdom of darkness, there are all forms of evil. All manner of sicknesses, afflictions, embarrassments, torments, and bad luck hold sway in this kingdom of darkness. All the people there are captives and are subject to all forms of evils. They have no source of help as long as they continue there. They are ruled and governed by the devil.

They are children of disobedience, and the devil continually lords it over them. They cannot protest. They have no right to. Their will has been submitted to the devil. They recognize him as their lord and master. They have become servants of sin.

> *Know ye not, that to whom ye yield yourselves servants to obey, his servants ye are to whom ye obey; whether of sin unto death, or of obedience unto righteousness?*
>
> Romans 6:16

They are held in bondage by the devil. He lords it over them because they have yielded themselves to him. But you are no longer under his control. You were delivered from that realm and state of servitude. Not only that, you were also translated into the kingdom of God Himself. You were brought out of darkness into light. You have become a partaker of the life and nature of the Father God.

There are four classes of beings in the spirit world. They are arranged in hierarchies. Note that you are a spirit being. A lot of people see themselves as merely physical. They are ignorant that they are spirit beings. God is a Spirit, he is not physical.

God is a Spirit: and they that worship him must worship him in spirit and in truth.

John 4:24

You have to understand this fact. God is a Spirit. He created man in His very image, a spirit being. Man essentially is a spirit. The person you see outside is not the man. The man on the inside is the real man. The figure you see outwardly is the house in which he lives. Man is in three dimensions. He is a spirit, has a soul, and lives in a body.

And the very God of peace sanctify you wholly; and I pray God your whole spirit and soul and body be preserved blameless unto the coming of our Lord Jesus Christ.

1 Thessalonians 5:23

Paul knew this fact very clearly. In his epistle to the Philippians, he told them of his indecision about whether to depart or continue to abide in the body.

But if I live in the flesh, this is the fruit of my labour: yet what I shall choose I wot not.

For I am in a strait betwixt two, having a desire to

48

depart, and to be with Christ; which is far better:

Nevertheless to abide in the flesh is more needful for you.

Philippians 1:22-24

Paul knew his make-up. He knew himself to be a spirit, and that the flesh is the house in which he "abides". Notice that there is a constant reference to "I." The "I" here is the real Paul, but the body (flesh) is his house. You are a spirit.

That which is born of the flesh is flesh; and that which is born of the Spirit is spirit.

John 3:6

You are born of God who is a Spirit. Therefore, you must be a spirit also. A man cannot give birth to a lizard, neither can a lizard give birth to a rat. An elephant will only reproduce after its kind, and God, when He gave birth to you, brought you forth a spirit.

So, there are four categories of beings in the spirit world. The one at the immediate base of the ladder is the class of unregenerated spirits. These are men that are not born again. They are still firmly in the hands of the devil as his servants. Their will and motives are directly under the control of demons and the devil. They are controlled by the spirit of the age. Can't you see how unbelievers do the most

49

unpardonable things? They commit the greatest blunders you can think of. They are influenced and motivated into that state by the devil. He has absolute right and control over their lives.

Immediately above this class is the demonic class. These are the angels that fell with the devil when God cast him out of heaven. They are called demons, and they operate against anything good in the world. They were once in the service of God. But they did not keep their former estate, so they were forcefully retired from God's host, without benefits. So they are not current with God's move. They are ignorant of kingdom truths. Their knowledge about God is obsolete. That is one of the reasons why Jesus said the gates of hell shall not be able to prevail against the church. They do not possess the manpower to carry it out.

The next set or class of spirits are God's holy angels. These are God's current soldiers. They are spirits who excel in strength. They occupy a higher realm than the devil and his demons. They are higher in status.

The highest class is God and His family. This is where you belong! You may ask me, "Brother David, do you mean I am higher in class than the angels?" My answer to you is an emphatic "yes." You cannot compare yourself with angels, as you are not on the same level. Angels are only created, but you are both created and regenerated. You have a better standing with God. Jesus did not die for angels; He died for you. They are your messengers. They are sent to minister to you.

> *But to which of the angels said he at any time, Sit on my right hand, until I make thine enemies thy footstool?*
>
> *Are they not all ministering spirits, sent forth to minister for them who shall be heirs of salvation?*
>
> Hebrews 1:13-14

Angels are your servants. That is why they are sent. The word "ministering spirits" is the same as "serving spirits." They are your servants in the spirit. They are not higher than you in class. God did not make you lower than angels. The word translated "angels" in Psalm 8:5 should have been translated God.

> *For thou hast made him a little lower than the angels, and hast crowned him with glory and honour.*
>
> Psalm 8:5

If you were created lower than angels, God would be unjust to make them your servants; because it is the lesser that serves the greater. If indeed they are higher, you should serve them. Get this point very clearly, and get hold of it.

When an angel appeared to John the beloved on the Island of Patmos, and John fell down to worship him, the angel protested and made a most revealing statement about their ministry to the believer.

Then saith he unto me, See thou do it not: for I am thy fellowservant, and of thy brethren the prophets, and of them which keep the sayings of this book: worship God.

Revelation 22:9

What the angel is saying there is that he is a fellow servant of God's people with John. You know the apostles consider themselves as servants. So the angel said, "I am also a servant of God's people. I am serving you presently. It is my duty to show you those things. I am performing my duty towards you." They serve us in all areas of life, including protection.

The angel of the LORD encampeth round about them that fear him, and delivereth them.

Psalm 34:7

They are the believer's Aide-de-camp. They attend to you in all areas of life.

So you are in God's class of being as a new creation.

You are accepted in the beloved. You are God's offspring, you are His loved son. You occupy a special place in His heart. You have His nature, His life, His Spirit, His faith, and His love. Everything about Him has been made available to you through the new creation. Therefore, it is not forgiveness of sin alone; it is comprehensive. You are exalted into the heavenly places, and seated there with Him.

> *But God, who is rich in mercy, for his great love wherewith he loved us,*
>
> *Even when we were dead in sins, hath quickened us together with Christ, (by grace ye are saved;)*
>
> *And hath raised us up together, and made us sit together in heavenly places in Christ Jesus.*
>
> Ephesians 2:4-6

You have become one with Christ. You are joined with Him. You have been given His very life - God's divine nature. You have been declared righteous, and have been restored to your former estate.

What you lost in Adam in the beginning, you have now regained in Christ. You have now been restored to your place of authority and dominion. You now hold sway over every situation in life, by virtue of your class of being. You are as invincible as God is. No devil can defeat you, if you stand in your proper position in God.

The nature and life of God is yours personally. You are new, and have been declared more than a conqueror.

There is an innate victory mentality in your nature, as God's nature is contrary to defeat and failure. He cannot fail, He does not have a sense of it. It is not possible with God! Look at it, God does not know failure, you are His son. God produces after His kind. You are in God's class, so, you are a god here on earth.

I have said, Ye are gods; and all of you are children of the most High.

Psalm 82:6

Jesus re-echoed this statement in the New Testament, thus affirming its authenticity. *"Jesus answered them, Is it not written in your law, I said, Ye are gods? (Jn. 10:34)."* Jesus said you are a god. Do not argue it, you are! Jesus said it. That puts you on victory plane. No enemy can overcome you, because you are a god. God has designed constant victory in your new status. It is over to you.

Note that the Lord Jesus has accomplished all these for you, making them yours legally. If you only stop at the legal possession without entering into it in reality, you will never get it. You will only have them credited into your account, but will never enjoy them; and so the devil will take advantage of you. But you can enter into it through faith in the finished work of Christ. God has designed faith as a basic requirement you must have and exercise to get anything from Him.

But without faith it is impossible to please him: for he that cometh to God must believe that he is, and that he is a rewarder of them that diligently seek him.

Hebrews 11:6

Your faith must please God for you to enter into your victory.

CHAPTER 4

THE FIGHT OF FAITH

The fight you are involved in is not physical. It is not a fight aimed at physical foes. You do not fight this battle in the arm of the flesh. It is fought with spiritual weapons.

For though we walk in the flesh, we do not war after the flesh:

for the weapons of our warfare are not carnal (phys- ical) but mighty through God to the pulling down of strongholds;

casting down imaginations, and every high thing that exalteth itself against the knowledge of God, and bringing into captivity every thought to the obe- dience of Christ.

2 Corinthians 10:3-5

The enemy you are warring against is not physical, so you cannot attack him with physical weapons. He is firing arrows (his fiery darts) at you. He is all out for you. So, you need to understand that the only way to stand against him is to resist him by faith.

The subject of faith cannot be over emphasized. It is one of the things that are indispensable in Christianity, which is a life of faith. As a matter of fact, Christianity is called, "The Faith." This is why a lot of emphasis has gone unto the faith message all over the world. You cannot amount to anything in Christianity without faith, for by grace you are saved through faith.

This faith business is very important. Some people ignorantly protest that the faith message is prevailing too much in the Church. Faith cannot be too much. It is the basis on which man relates with God. Without it, man cannot get anything from God. So He has designed that man must live by faith, to justify his divine nature. God is a faith God, and for anybody to live up to His expectation, he has to live by faith too.

In this fight, your faith is in direct conflict with the devil. The enemy knows that you are what your faith is. The quality of your life also depends entirely on your faith. You will never get any victory that is bigger than your faith.

Note that God has done everything on His own side. He has completed His own part of the contract. He has exalted you legally, and has completed your every moment victory in the Lord Jesus Christ. But He expects you to enter into them and cause them to be real in your everyday life, by faith.

He is expecting His enemies to be subject to you. So the enemy is constantly warring against you to make sure that your faith is weakened. If he can cause your faith to dwindle, he has got you. Your faith is the fortress that keeps the devil off your territory. If you are in faith, the devil knows that he is in a danger zone. Jesus told Simon Peter that the devil was planning against him, but He had prayed that Peter's faith would not fail. That is what the enemy is about. He wants your faith to fail. He wants you battered out of shape.

And the Lord said, Simon, Simon, behold, Satan hath desired to have you, that he may sift you as wheat:

But I have prayed for thee, that thy faith fail not...

Luke 22:31-32

Jesus did not pray that Satan would not desire Peter, or that Peter would not be tempted. He knew it is normal to be tempted by the devil. That is his major occupation. If he does not tempt, who else would? So Jesus did not find any wisdom in praying against temptation. Instead, He prayed that Peter's faith would not fail. It shows how important your faith life is. It makes the difference between victory and defeat. It means that if Peter's faith failed, the devil could get him; but if it did not, there was no way the devil could get at him. Your faith is Satan's target, because that is what you use in resisting him.

> *Be sober, be vigilant; because your adversary the devil, as a roaring lion, walketh about, seeking whom he may devour:*
>
> *Whom resist stedfast in the faith, knowing that the same afflictions are accomplished in your brethren that are in the world.*
>
> 1 Peter 5:8-9

Do you see now that you resist the devil by your faith? He cannot get you until he has gotten your faith. Your faith is a menace to him.

> *Above all, taking the shield of faith, wherewith ye shall be able to quench all the fiery darts of the wicked.*
>
> Ephesians 6:16

When the devil comes with his problems, it is your duty to ward off his assaults with the shield of faith.

When he comes with sickness, you use your faith to resist it. Your victory can only be won and sustained by faith. There is no other way to it, for God has designed it so.

It is also important for you to know that it is your faith that will win this battle for you. It is not your pastor's or any of your fellowship leaders'. It is your own faith in the victory of Christ that makes the difference.

Behold, his soul which is lifted up is not upright in him: but the just shall live by his faith.

Habakkuk 2:4

Get hold of this truth. It is your faith that will put you over in all life's difficulties. When the enemy comes, it is your faith that will see you through. This is so important that it is mentioned four times in the entire Bible.

For therein is the righteousness of God revealed from faith to faith: as it is written, The just shall live by faith.

Romans 1:17

...For, The just shall live by faith.

Galatians 3:11

Now the just shall live by faith: but if any man draw back, my soul shall have no pleasure in him.

Hebrews 10:38

There is no compromise about it. Your own faith is the key to your personal victory. Most of the fights you will ever have to fight are personal. Not many of them are collective. Even those that are collective still have personal effects. So for you to really win in any of them, your faith must be out there working very well.

The people that Jesus healed in the scriptures received their healings on the basis of their personal faith. It was not the faith of Jesus that healed them, but their own faith. The woman with the issue of blood got her victory by her own faith.

She had determined to be healed. I believe that woman had fought one of the toughest battles anybody can fight on earth. She had an issue of blood consistently for 12 years. She had spent everything she had, but no improvement was visible. Jesus did not even notice her in the crowd, but she forced her way through the great press to touch His garment. She did not want to know how much of the garment she could touch. Even the hem alone was enough to secure her healing, and she got it.

> *But Jesus turned him about, and when he saw her, he said, Daughter, be of good comfort; thy faith hath made thee whole. And the woman was made whole from that hour.*
>
> Matthew 9:22

When Jesus healed two blind men in that same chapter of Matthew, He mentioned that it was the believer's personal faith that gets the victory.

> *And when he was come into the house, the blind men came to him: and Jesus saith unto them, Believe ye that I am able to do this? They said unto him, Yea, Lord.*
>
> *Then touched he their eyes, saying, According to your faith be it unto you.*
>
> Matthew 9:28-29

That has always been the precedent. No man receives anything from God without faith. He must see faith before He moves on your behalf. Faith is essential for personal victory. Paul was preaching in Lystra, where an impotent man was in the audience. He was impotent in his feet from his mother's womb. He could not walk, because he was a cripple.

> *The same heard Paul speak: who stedfastly beholding him, and perceiving that he had faith to be healed,*
>
> *Said with a loud voice, Stand upright on thy feet. And he leaped and walked.*
>
> Acts 14:9-10

It is easy to say that Paul healed the man who had

been crippled from his mother's womb. But the Bible says, *"he had faith to be healed"*. If he did not have faith for healing, his victory would not have come at that time. Notice also that the man leaped and walked by himself.

You need faith for your victory. The point is that your victory has been made certain. It has been completed; it is a foregone conclusion. But you need to personally appropriate your faith to get into it. That is the faith that gets the job done.

The problem with most people is that, instead of walking by faith, they choose to walk by sight. The Bible says the just shall live by his faith, not by sight. It is amazing to see people set all their attention on their problems. They so focus on it, until it is magnified above their imagination.

They are like a young man who sees a cat. He gets so engulfed in thinking about the cat, that he eventually gets himself into believing the cat to be a lion, and he exclaims, "Behold a lion!" Yet the supposed lion is just a cat. He magnified it.

People have magnified their problems above what they are. They depend solely on their five senses. They only believe those things they can see around them. They depend on their senses of sight, smell, taste, touch and hearing. Outside these, they cannot operate. But

God intends for you to walk by faith, and not by sight.

For we walk by faith, not by sight

2 Corinthians 5:7

The new creation man that you are is not designed to walk by his five senses. You are not ordinary; you are special. There is a world of difference between you and the natural man you can see around you. Your own content and quality of life is different. You are a new specie. A kind of you has never existed.

You have been brought into oneness with God, so you have to walk like him. God is a faith God. He is your Father. He is a faith Father, so you are supposed to be a faith son. If you walk by sight, you will operate outside your natural style of life. God demonstrated His faith lifestyle in His creation programme. God created the earth by faith.

Through faith we understand that the worlds were framed by the word of God, so that things which are seen were not made of things which do appear.

Hebrews 11:3

God was basically on a faith project here. He framed the worlds from things that are not visible. He was not walking by sight, He walked by faith.

65

He used His eyes of faith, and it worked. He has designed the same system for you to operate in. If you follow God in the life of faith, you will get God's success results. It cannot fail.

It is by walking by faith that you will overcome all difficulties and win your battles always. Your victory is always guaranteed, but note that you cannot enter into it except you walk by faith.

> *For whatsoever is born of God overcometh the world: and this is the victory that overcometh the world, even our faith.*

1 John 5:4

There is no victory outside faith. It is not a physical battle which you can easily win if you are hefty and muscular. It is not by power or might, but by the Spirit of the Lord. That is why the Bible says it is by faith you stand. Faith is essential. It is as vital as breathing. Without faith you cannot please God. It will take faith for you to be on your feet.

> *Not for that we have dominion over your faith, but are helpers of your joy: for by faith ye stand.*

2 Corinthians 1:24

If you are on your feet, then you are in victory. So it is by faith that you can stay an overcomer.

Walk by faith!

CHAPTER 5

A BORN WINNER

By virtue of your birth, you have been declared a winner. You have a winner covenant with God the Father. He has destined you to win. You are not meant for failure and defeat, but for great exploits in victory. There is no fight, however fierce, no battle, however tough, that you cannot overcome. You can have as many victories as the battles you have, as long as you abide in God and know Him intimately. With this, your degree of exploits is unlimited, because:

...The people that do know their God shall be strong, and do exploits.

Daniel 11:32

The children of Israel knew this secret. From Abraham we notice that no man, nation, or a conspiracy of nations was able to defeat them in any battle. God called Abraham and gave him a covenant. He told him He would bless his seed and make them great. He signed the covenant of prosperity, health, strength, and constant victory with Abraham on behalf of Israel.

A very important truth about God is His faithfulness. If He has said a thing, He is bound to perform it. He is a sticker to His word. He can never be drawn into any situation that will make Him break His word. He is not a man that He should lie, neither is He a son of man that He should change His mind about His word. Check it up with God, and notice that He will always stand by His word to fulfill it. He gives priority to the fulfillment of the word. The word is His expressed will.

> *God is not a man, that he should lie; neither the son of man, that he should repent: hath he said, and shall he not do it? or hath he spoken, and shall he not make it good?*

Numbers 23:19

Such is God's faithfulness to His covenant. He is a covenant-keeping God. You cannot make Him break His word. Even if man disappoints Him, He cannot deny Himself. He is God.

> *...He will ever be mindful of his covenant.*

Psalm 111:5

He sent redemption unto his people: he hath commanded his covenant for ever: holy and reverend is his name.

Psalm 111:9

The people of Israel know this about God. They are God's covenant people. The Bible describes them as the church in the wilderness (Acts 7:38). They went through all their battles successfully, with absolute victory. No battle was lost when they were in right relationship with God.

The drama in Egypt is most illuminating. God had appeared to Moses and commissioned him to lead His people out of the house of bondage. After consulting with the elders of the people, Moses went to Pharaoh to demand Israel's unconditional release. It was a mighty conflict; perhaps the greatest ever recorded in history. Pharaoh refused, and the battle began.

It was not necessarily a battle or fight between Moses and Pharaoh, but a battle between the true God and the god of Egypt. It was so, because God had to act on the basis of His covenant with Abraham. God had told Abraham that his seed would go into a foreign land to sojourn where they would be oppressed, but that He would bring them out with a mighty hand.

And he said unto Abram, Know of a surety that thy seed shall be a stranger in a land that is not theirs, and shall serve them; and they shall afflict them four hundred years;

And also that nation, whom they shall serve, will I judge: and afterward shall they come out with great substance.

Genesis 15:13-14

God proved Himself great on behalf of Israel in Egypt. The people of Israel won all the battles. They did not lose any, so long as they walked with God. The Bible has a comprehensive catalogue of these victories. It is really an eye opener to consider the winning life-style of Israel. They centered on the basis of God's covenant of victory; and had it always. God caused them to triumph always.

After God had proved Himself to Pharaoh and all Egypt, and had delivered them by a mighty hand, with signs and great wonders, the people of Israel set out on their journey with great substance. They left the land of Egypt with goods, cattle, and all good things. Great was God's goodness to them.

As they progressed in their journey, Pharaoh felt he had made a mistake by allowing them to go. So he brought all his men of valour together, along with

70

the sophistication of his army; virtually the best in the world at that time, and started on a hot chase of God's people, to destroy them. He took six hundred chosen chariots, and all the chariots of Egypt, and captains over each of them. He really prepared to finish God's people. He knew that they had taken the wilderness route, and that the Red Sea was there. So he had finalized his plans to destroy Israel. His heart was hardened; he was determined.

> *But the Egyptians pursued after them, all the horses and chariots of Pharaoh, and his horsemen, and his army, and overtook them encamping by the sea, beside Pihahiroth, before Baalzephon.*
>
> Exodus 14:9

This was the first battle they were going to face since leaving Egypt. It was almost too early for them to begin to encounter such conflicts.

They had an unsettling problem before them. The Red Sea was there, a great obstacle indeed. They had not found an answer to that yet, and here was the great host of Egypt. Pharaoh brought all his army, chariots, captains and horsemen against a physically unarmed Israel.

Naturally, that was a dark hour for them. They had a battle on hand – a tough one. They could not run away. Miraculously, the Red Sea gave way as Moses used his rod, and the children of Israel crossed over to the other side, on dry ground; but both Pharaoh and his men got drowned in the sea.

> ***Thus the LORD saved Israel that day out of the hand of the Egyptians; and Israel saw the Egyptians dead upon the sea shore.***
>
> Exodus 14:30

This was Israel's first deliverance. Nothing touched any of them, but the whole army of Pharaoh perished in that fight.

The people of Israel moved, taking on their journey. When they got to the land of the Amorites, they sent a message to Sihon their king, to allow them pass through their land peacefully. They did not mean to fight. They were not looking for trouble with the people, all they wanted was just a free passage.

When God is on your side, you do not go about looking for trouble. You know your right as an over-comer. A champion does not go about challenging people. He knows he is superior to all other fighters. So they wanted free passage through the land of the Amorites.

> ***And Israel sent messengers unto Sihon king of the Amorites, saying,***

Let me pass through thy land: we will not turn into the fields, or into the vineyards; we will not drink of the waters of the well: but we will go along by the king's high way, until we be past thy borders.

Numbers 21:21-22

But funny enough, the Amorites refused them passage. Instead, they marshalled all their men together, and fought Israel. Sihon took his people into the wilderness to fight against Israel. Israel, however, stood against them, and defeated them very neatly.

And Israel smote him with the edge of the sword, and possessed his land from Arnon unto Jabbok, even unto the children of Ammon: for the border of the children of Ammon was strong.

Numbers 21:24

They marched on from victory onto victory. There was no nation that could stand against them. They made a mess of Jericho, Ai, king Og, and the Amorites – the five kings.

They won all their battles. Jericho was reported to be one of the strongest cities in the world at that time. Their security was the best. The city wall was strong and mighty. History has it that the wall of Jericho was so thick that six horsemen could ride side-by-side with ease on it. It was so thick that Rahab the harlot could build her house on it. The wall of Jericho was strong enough to accommodate a whole house. *"for her house was upon the town wall, and she dwelt upon the wall"* (Joshua 2:15).

But this wall could not stand the covenant people. Apart from the wall, the land of Jericho had men of valour in it. They were mighty men of valour (Joshua 6:2). But when they heard of the covenant people, their hearts melted. They knew no one could prevail against these people.

The children of Israel knew their covenant right to victory. So everybody that came against them went down. Jericho's wall, with all its mighty men of valour, perished. They were born victors and winners.

As they progressed, kingdoms and nations heard about their exploits. Their hearts melted in them. They were helpless, and so started looking for help from other kingdoms. They formed a conspiracy against Israel, but they all fell.

The five kings of the Amorites are a classical example here. Adonizedec, king of Jerusalem, had heard that Gibeon made peace with Israel. So he sent messages to Hoham, king of Hebron, Piram, king of Jarmuth Japhia, king of Lachish, and Debir, king of Eglon, to help him fight against Gibeon. Gibeon, on the other hand, sent quickly to Joshua for help. Joshua came up in defence of Gibeon, and smote the confederacy of the Amorites. He utterly destroyed all of them, and none of the children of Israel was hurt in the battle.

Throughout their wilderness experience, whenever they were in fellowship with God, they won all their battles. Joshua led the people of God to overcome about thirty-one kings and kingdoms. They did not lose to any of them.

God had earlier made a covenant with Abraham about these people. When God met him initially, He made fantastic promises to him and his seed after him.

> *I will make of thee a great nation, and I will bless thee, and make thy name great; and thou shalt be a blessing: And I will bless them that bless thee, and curse him that curseth thee: and in thee shall all families of the earth be blessed.*
>
> Genesis 12:2-3

Whoever blessed Israel got blessed, and whoever cursed them got cursed. There was an automatic curse upon any and every enemy of Israel. God is bound by His covenant to protect their interest all the time. Take time to read Joshua chapter twelve, and see Israel's catalogue of triumphs. No kingdom was strong enough to stand against them. They all fell easy prey to Joshua and his people.

It is still the same today with that small nation of Israel. Geographically, they are not a force, but in other aspects, they rank number one in the world today. No nation can stop them. The Arab League are mere noise makers beside Israel. Look at the six days' war. There is no precedence of that. A conglomeration of powerful nations invading a small piece of land, but instead got finished within six days.

Even the United Nations cannot stop Israel on any issue. They have God's covenant. They declared "Jerusalem the eternal and indivisible capital of Israel" sometime ago. The whole world protested. The United Nations passed a resolution against it, but nothing else could be done about it.

God is in that nation. They have God's word for that. That is why they can boast of victory any day. They do not live by what is said about them in the international circles; they stick with God's covenant with Abraham, Isaac, Jacob, and David – king of Israel.

Many of the nations that have severed relations with them are now turning around to acknowledge God in their midst.

The fact remains that any nation that stands against Israel is politically and economically against God's channel of blessings. I believe very strongly that Nigeria's only solution is to normalize relations with Israel, and she will be healed of her economic and political problems.

Most importantly, Israel is a type of the Church. Israel was the Church in the wilderness. They are a shadow of the true Church, the body of believers. Believers are the real Israel.

> *For the law having a shadow of good things to come, and not the very image of the things, can never with those sacrifices which they offered year by year continually make the comers thereunto perfect.*
>
> Hebrews 10:1

Every truth in the Old Testament is a figure, a type, a shadow of some real things in the New Testament. The children of Israel were a picture of the believers under the new covenant.

They enjoyed those victories on the basis of the covenant received by Abraham, which was sealed with the blood of bulls and goats. That covenant also belongs to us and Jesus came to consecrate a better covenant with His blood.

We are the true Israelites. Although God is still

committed to Israel after the flesh, we are the very Israel of God. We are God's chosen people. The promise God gave Abraham was that He would make his seed after him great. He would bless his seed, and they shall be mighty, and no situation would be too strong for them to overcome. As a matter of fact, they were overcomers and victors by virtue of birth and parentage.

They are overcomers and winners in every fight because they are the physical seed of Abraham. God has also made you one at new birth. He has imparted His seed nature into you, which changed you from being a Gentile, into a bonafide seed of Abraham. Your new identity is based on your wholehearted acceptance of the sacrifice of Christ and His victory on the cross. That qualifies you to be Christ's. So you are Abraham's seed.

> *Christ hath redeemed us from the curse of the law, being made a curse for us: for it is written, Cursed is every one that hangeth on a tree:*
>
> *That the blessing of Abraham might come on the Gentiles through Jesus Christ; that we might receive the promise of the Spirit through faith.*
>
> *Now to Abraham and his seed were the promises made. He saith not, And to seeds, as of many; but as of one, And to thy seed, which is Christ.*
>
> Galatians 3:13, 14, 16

Christ went to the cross, that you might receive the blessings of Abraham. The blessings were sworn to Abraham and his seed in the covenant. If you must partake of the blessings, you must come under the covenant. Moreover, the covenant was made to Abraham and his seed. Christ is the seed we are talking about. If you belong to Christ, you are the promise, and you are covered under the covenant.

And if ye be Christ's, then are ye Abraham's seed, and heirs according to the promise.

Galatians 3:29

This is very clear. You come under this victory covenant. You are the Israel of God, as it is not the physical Israel only that is God's real Israel.

For he is not a Jew, which is one outwardly; neither is that circumcision, which is outward in the flesh:

But he is a Jew, which is one inwardly; and circumcision is that of the heart, in the spirit, and not in the letter; whose praise is not of men, but of God.

Romans 2:28-29

Not as though the word of God hath taken none effect. For they are not all Israel, which are of Israel:

Neither, because they are the seed of Abraham, are they all children: but, In Isaac shall thy seed be called.

Romans 9:6-7

God still has a legal commitment to keep His covenant with natural Israel; but His commitment to you is both legal and vital.

The point is that many believers have underrated themselves. They do not seem to understand their true standing before God. These children of Israel are the children of the flesh. Their relationship with Abraham and the covenant is based on physical inheritance alone. But you are the spiritual Israel. God is more eager to prove His victory covenant to you than He will to Israel. The covenant you have cannot be broken. He is bound to give you the victory always.

There is no limit to what He will do to give you the victory. You cannot number how many people, nations and kingdoms God killed to bring victory to the physical Israel. God is committed to your success and victory much more.

It does not matter what the situation is, if you see God doing anything for the nation of Israel, He will do much more for you. You are His very seed. You are His partner in the covenant. You are the apple of His eyes. Stop relegating yourself. God is against anybody that is against you, and against anything that is against you.

People have to be careful the way they treat believers.

You cannot just toy with God's precious people. God will not throw His precious people to the swine. Jesus said no man gives anything precious to pigs. God will not allow you to be tossed around by anybody, group, government or authority. You are a sensitive matter in God's programme. There is a "touch not" decree on you, based on the covenant.

> *He is the LORD our God: his judgments are in all the earth.*
>
> *He hath remembered his covenant for ever, the word which he commanded to a thousand generations.*
>
> *Which covenant he made with Abraham, and his oath unto Isaac;*
>
> *And confirmed the same unto Jacob for a law, and to Israel for an everlasting covenant:*
>
> *When they went from one nation to another, from one kingdom to another people;*
>
> *He suffered no man to do them wrong: yea, he reproved kings for their sakes;*
>
> *Saying, Touch not mine anointed, and do my prophets no harm.*
>
> Psalm 105:7-10, 13-15

His covenant is forever. He is mindful of it. He did not allow anybody to do them wrong. God is not interested in you being messed around and treated anyhow. He does not want it. It is not part of the covenant. Those who attempted to wrong the people of Israel paid dearly for it.

Those who attempted evil against Moses even in the camp of Israel paid for it. Do not allow things to go anyhow with you. There is a pattern which God has designed for you.

God reproved kings for the sake of the people of Israel. Kings! He will reprove kings for your sake too. I do not know a man who will allow straying objects to touch the apple of his eyes. Yet God says you are the apples of His eyes. He will do anything to protect you, even if it means killing.

> *For thus saith the LORD of hosts; After the glory hath he sent me unto the nations which spoiled you: for he that toucheth you toucheth the apple of his eye.*
>
> *For, behold, I will shake mine hand upon them, and they shall be a spoil to their servants: and ye shall know that the LORD of hosts hath sent me.*
>
> Zechariah 2:8-9

Nobody can take advantage of you and go free. That "touch not" statement is a command, a decree. It carries certain penalties if broken. Know this, that you are born of God. He is interested in your winning always. If the physical Israel can win all their battles with impunity, you can do much more than that, because you are born of God.

For whatsoever is born of God overcometh the world: and this is the victory that overcometh the world, even our faith.

1 John 5:4

You can overcome always! The greater One is in you. He is at work in you now. He is greater than all your life battles, so you can win them all. He is working His good pleasure in you. You are a born winner!

CHAPTER 6

GETTING SET FOR YOUR VICTORY

There are three basic steps to getting set for your miracle. If you take time to observe them and prepare yourself with them, they will get you to a place of readiness for victory. They are:

1. Keep to your source

2. Be still

3. The act of praise

KEEP TO YOUR SOURCE

You are required to know your source, and to keep only to it. Note that *"God is a jealous God"* (Exodus 20:5). He cannot stand a double deal. He cannot perform for people who stand between two opinions. That is wavering. That is doubt. Your expectation is either only from Him, or you are not ready for His great acts at all. The Psalmist says:

> *My soul, wait thou only upon God; for my expectation is from him.*
>
> Psalm 62:5

That is how to get started. God "will not give his glory to another, neither His praise to graven images" (Isaiah 42:8).

The reason for this double dealing is not far fetched. People think God must of necessity have to go through some men to accomplish His word. No sir! God is all sufficient. He is El-Shaddai. He is God that is more than enough to meet all needs, all by Himself. He may go through animate and inanimate objects for, He said, "I can command stones to praise me." Jesus brought food to 5,000 directly from above (John 6). God was replenishing the widow of Zarephath's pot of flour and the cruise of oil all by Himself (1 Kings 17). He may choose to use a man; but it is not a must.

Be sure you are waiting only upon Him, then you will be setting your feet on the miracle-line. Know that your God will not stand double dealing. Know also that He is up to all situations that may ever arise in your life. He is omnipotent. But double deal can put Him off your matter.

There was the case of a woman I was ministering to for a miracle. God ministered to me in the course of laying on of hands, "This woman has an alternative." I stopped the prayer and told the woman, "God said you have an alternative source for what you are seeking. True or false?" She affirmed in the positive. Then I told her she should make up her mind who to choose; the living God or her poor alternative. I gave her some time, instructing her that when she was through, she should send for me. That was enough reason for the Most High to fold His hands. He is a jealous God. He wants all the glory of every matter. The Bible says:

> *They looked unto him, and were lightened: and their faces were not ashamed.*
>
> Psalm 34:5

The word further enjoins:

> *...If therefore thine eye be single, thy whole body shall be full of light.*
>
> Matthew 6:22

Look unto the hills, your help is sure awaiting you. Look not unto Moses, look unto the serpent of bronze hung in the centre of the congregation; look, and you will live. If any Israelite was looking elsewhere when bitten by a serpent, no matter to whom, he would surely die (Numbers 21). Look unto Him only, and you will live.

BE STILL

The Bible says:

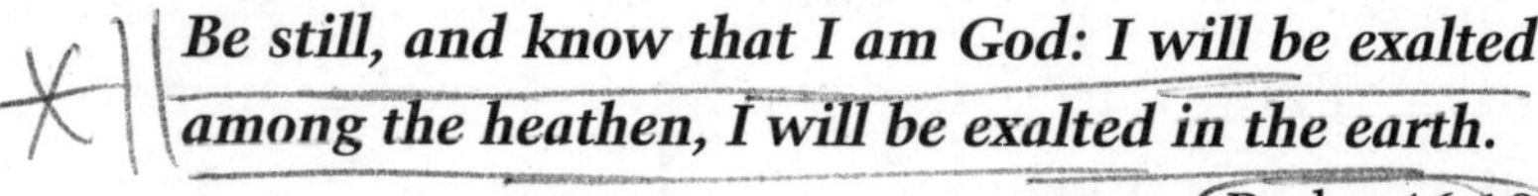

Be still, and know that I am God: I will be exalted among the heathen, I will be exalted in the earth.

Psalm 46:10

This is a vital requirement for walking in the realm of the miraculous. Many miss God's best through anxiety and haste, which the word likens to foolishness.

There was the case of Saul the son of kish, the King of Israel. Samuel the prophet was to be around to offer sacrifices on behalf of the land. They waited for him, but after a while Saul decided to offer the sacrifices. Behold, as soon as he had finished with the sacrifices, Samuel arrived, and it was counted to Saul for foolishness. The Bible says you have no cause for haste, as *"He that believeth shall not make haste"* (Isaiah 28:16).

You have no reason for anxiety. The word says:

Which of you by taking thought can add one cubit

unto his stature?

And why take ye thought for raiment? Consider the lilies of the field, how they grow; they toil not, neither do they spin.

Matthew 6:27-28

You must hands off the matter completely before God will take over.

The LORD shall fight for you, and ye shall hold your peace.

Exodus 14:14

The reason God is so far from many believers today is that they will not hold their peace. It is written:

...In quietness and in confidence shall be your strength: and ye would not.

But ye said, No; for we will flee upon horses; therefore shall ye flee: and, We will ride upon the swift; therefore shall they that pursue you be swift.

Isaiah 30:15-16

Again it is written:

...I cried concerning this, Their strength is to sit still.

Isaiah 30:7

If really you are targeting a miraculous life, you must be still. It is in your quietness that you are able to catch the "still small voice", then you will have your miracle. There was the story of Elijah the prophet in 1 Kings 19. When he was complaining and murmuring, he had no solution to his problems. But as he laid down quietly, the still small voice came, and that gave him the way out. You cannot afford to be hysterical if you must lay hold on your miracles.

THE ACT OF PRAISE

O give thanks unto the Lord; for he is good: for his mercies endureth forever.

Psalm 136:1

The subject of praise is a very vital issue that everyone expecting a miracle must understand. The Bible says praise is comely unto God (Psalm 147:1). God desires the praises of His people. And this is the reason why *"God inhabits the praises of His people"* (Psalm 22:3).

A praise-filled life is surely a miracle-packed life. Praise brings God right into your situation. God deals directly with praise, while angels run the errand of prayers. Praise gets you right into God's presence. It is written:

Enter into his gates with thanksgiving, and into his courts with praise: be thankful unto him, and bless his name.

Psalm 100:4

What a revelation! *In God's presence there is fullness of joy, and on His right hand are pleasures forevermore* (Psalm 16:11).

Praise will get you across to Zion, where *there shall be deliverance and holiness, and the house of Jacob shall possess their possessions* (Obadiah 17).

Zion is the city of the living God, the domain of miracles. The Bible says, *"But ye are come unto mount Sion, and unto the city of the living God, the heavenly Jerusalem, and to an innumerable company of angels, to the general assembly and church of the firstborn, which are written in heaven, and to God the Judge of all, and to the spirits of just men made perfect"* (Hebrews 12:22-23).

That is why mount Zion is a mount of miracles, and praise is what gets you there. Praise gets you directly to where God lives, and in His presence there is fullness of joy, and pleasures forevermore.

The Bible says:

Let the people praise thee, O God; let all the people praise thee.

Then shall the earth yield her increase; and God, even our own God, shall bless us.

91

God shall bless us; and all the ends of the earth shall fear him.

Psalm 67:5-7

That is supernatural blessing, miraculous blessing. Men who are possessed with praise are entitled to such wonders. Praise gets the devil out of the scene, and brings God there. Remember how David was casting out devils by playing his divine music on a stringed instrument (1 Samuel 16:23).

No devil can stand the force of genuine praise and worship. Such place is exclusively reserved for God. God has the monopoly of praise centres. If you are a praise-filled believer, you will keep the devil constantly at a distance from your environment. Why do you suppose that the year of jubilee is the year of restoration? It is because when there is jubilation, praise and worship, God is ever set to perform wonders (Leviticus 25). The Lord is fearful in praises (Exodus 15:11).

Bring out praises from your heart, and you will get God to go full-length in performing for you. Clouds get lifted up during praise. Elisha the prophet said, "Bring me a minstrel, let's get the cloud cleared." Praises cleared the cloud, and a bright revelation came

(2 Kings 3:15). That is praise at work.

A merry heart doeth good like a medicine.

Proverbs 17:22

Possess a merry heart of praise and bag your miracles.

SECTION TWO

Steps To Victory

There are seven important steps to victory, which the next chapters focus on. These steps will work for anybody, anywhere, because they have their root in God, and are centred around the word of God.

The word of God does not know cultural or geographical barriers. It is constant. It works anywhere and everywhere it is rightly applied, the devil notwithstanding. Study these steps carefully, and stick to them meticulously, and your victory will be real.

CHAPTER 7

GET HOLD OF THE WORD

God has said something about that area of your life in which you desire victory, but it is your responsibility to search it out. The Bible says:

My people are destroyed for lack of knowledge...

Hosea 4:6

That you are a child of God alone does not guarantee your victory. You need personal knowledge of what God has said. Knowledge, they say, is power. The knowledge of God's word that you have about your situation will make you a victor. It will bring you to a place of faith in God's ability, and in your well-purchased victory.

> *...Far be it from God, that he should do wickedness; and from the Almighty, that he should commit iniquity.*
>
> *Surely it is meet to be said unto God, I have borne chastisement, I will not offend any more:*
>
> *That which I see not teach thou me: if I have done iniquity, I will do no more.*

Job 34:10, 31-32

This implies that evil comes through two main ways into a believer's life – sin and ignorance.

Of the two, ignorance is more serious and pathetic. The sinning believer can easily be motivated to repent, but ignorance is a deadly enemy of victory. If you are ignorant of God's word in a particular situation, the best you will likely do is to explain it away, believing that it is God's will.

There was a time my son, David Junior's temperature started rising. This feverish condition persisted for two days. He began to vomit his food and suffered sleeplessness. People said the symptom was normal, because he would soon develop his upper milk teeth. I said to myself that if that was so then it was necessary I set myself to find out what God has to say concerning children whose upper teeth are developing. That may sound funny, but that was the wisest thing to do.

A believer who wants to see good days should not take the world's views of things at face value. He must probe into the truth of such views with the word of God which is the final authority on all issues of life. This is a necessary step to walking in victory.

I gave myself to the study of the word, with the aid of a concordance. I discovered that the Bible does not say that the development of a child's milk teeth should be accompanied by feverish condition, sleeplessness and vomiting.

I went on to study in particular about the welfare of believers' children and, and a great refreshing came over me. The Holy Spirit began to illuminate my heart with the revelation of the relevant scriptures. I discovered that *"Children are an heritage (blessing)of the LORD; and that The blessing of the LORD, it maketh rich, and he addeth no sorrow with it"* (Psa. 127:3; Prov. 10:22

I discovered also that my child has an angel that owes him a protection duty. The word says:

...Their angels do always behold the face of my Father

which is in heaven.

Matthew 18:10

Also, assurance is given that:

...I will contend with him that contendeth with thee, and I will save thy children.

Isaiah 49:25

I needed no better assurances than these. I became victory-conscious on the issue at that stage.

You may ask, "How does one get to the point of personal knowledge of the word?" In other words, "How does one get to know from the word what rightly belongs to him?"

First of all, you must agree with yourself that you require such personal knowledge. It is the soil in which faith germinates. The Bible says, *"The just shall live by (his own) faith."*

Jesus said often; *"According to your faith be it unto you."* This means that how much you receive from God depends on how much you believe Him for. Personal faith is the answer, as another person's faith cannot offer you lasting victory over your personal issues. Brethren can only help you up to a point by their faith. But you have got to be able to stand on your own feet to fight your own battles.

Since *"faith cometh by hearing"* (knowledge), you require personal knowledge of the word before you can exercise it.

CHAPTER 8

RELEASE YOUR FAITH

Faith is an important prerequisite to receiving your personal victory. Your faith in Him pleases Him the same way your confidence in the promises of your earthly father pleases him and encourages him to strive to make himself worthy of such esteem.

Unless every word is mixed with faith, it cannot work. Paul said:

> *For unto us was the gospel preached, as well as unto them: but the word preached did not profit them, not being mixed with faith in them that heard it.*
>
> Hebrews 4:2

It takes meditation to get the word mixed with faith.

Meditation is an exercise involving the heart. The heart must open up to receive the revelation of the word through the service of the Holy Spirit.

The Church today seems to have missed this important aspect of the Christian faith. There is no real meditation in the word of God. The Bible has become a dusty book on the bookshelves, of many people professing to be believers. They only hurry through a few verses in the morning, read through one or two chapters on Sunday, and neatly tuck it back on their shelves. "That is enough with God for the day," they will mutter to themselves. Then they will plunge into their daily business activities and preoccupations with zeal, believing that the blessings of God would continue to follow them.

But the word says:

This book of the law shall not depart out of thy mouth; but thou shalt meditate therein day and night, that thou mayest observe to do according to all that is written therein: for then thou shalt make thy way prosperous, and then thou shalt have good success.

Joshua 1:8

Again in Psalm 1:1-3, it is written:

Blessed is the man that walketh not in the counsel

of the ungodly, nor standeth in the way of sinners, nor sitteth in the seat of the scornful.

But his delight is in the law of the LORD; and in his law doth he meditate day and night.

And he shall be like a tree planted by the rivers of water, that bringeth forth his fruit in his season; his leaf also shall not wither; and whatsoever he doeth shall prosper.

The art of meditation is, therefore, not a hurried business, or a weekly affair that takes place in the chapel. It should be a continual exercise in the daily walk of the believer. The blessed man the Psalmist talks about has not only delighted himself in the word of God, but he has also given himself to genuine meditation in it.

If you meet a believer whose life reflects victory, you have seen someone who meditates on the word of God on a constant basis.

There are three things that make for effective meditation. I have mentioned the part played by the Holy Spirit as the divine teacher. The rest are time, and right company. You need time to ponder on the Word before proceeding to appropriate it in the particular circumstance. In the case of my son, David Jnr., I had to create time to study and meditate upon the word. Then my faith started forming around the promises, until I got to a point where I knew that the Word would work for me.

I must say at this point that meditation consists in spiritual searching of the mysteries backing the Word. This is not within the human capacity to handle, for *"No man knoweth the things of God except the Spirit of God."* I had to be aided by the Holy Spirit.

An atmosphere of perverse talk, riotous living and other forms of immoral behaviour will not help you to meditate in the word of God. There is no way you can profitably engage in it. You need a quiet and sound atmosphere to motivate you into a life of profitable meditation in the word. The Bible declares:

> **Blessed is the man that walketh not in the counsel of the ungodly, nor standeth in the way of sinners, nor sitteth in the seat of the scornful.**
>
> Psalm 1:1

Paul warned, *"bad company ruins good morals."* Christ gave a similar warning:

> **Give not that which is holy unto the dogs, neither cast ye your pearls before swine, lest they trample them under their feet, and turn again and rend you.**
>
> Matthew 7:6

Productive meditation is hindered when you are in the midst of bad company. In fact, in that situation you are in danger of being influenced.

He that walketh with wise men shall be wise: but a companion of fools shall be destroyed.

Proverbs 13:20

Definitely, wrong company has robbed many believers of God's perfect plan for their lives. If you are a believer, avoid sitting in the wrong places, else you are sure to operate a wrong counsel and walk in the wrong path.

Therefore, you need to give yourself to the study of the Word.

Study to shew thyself approved unto God, a workman that needeth not to be ashamed, rightly dividing the word of truth.

2 Timothy 2:15

There is no short-cut to acquiring knowledge. The scriptures are not to be read for excitement and vocabulary alone as they are spirit and life. You therefore require in-depth study to acquire in-depth knowledge of the mysteries contained therein.

Moreover, you need revelation knowledge of the Word through the ministration of the Holy Spirit.

The Holy Spirit is the divine Teacher. It is written that when He (Holy Spirit) is come:

> *...**He shall teach you all things, and bring all things to your remembrance**...*

John 14:26

The Holy Spirit has a two-fold ministry here. He teaches the Word by imparting revelation knowledge; He sheds light on it, turning it into a voice. That is why the Bible is the voice of God – *"I know my sheep, they know my voice."*

The Holy Spirit also brings to remembrance whatever He teaches when it is required for use. He reminds you of the counsel of God you have come across in the word. He knows the mind of God on every issue, because:

> *...**God hath revealed them unto us by his Spirit: for the Spirit searcheth all things, yea, the deep things of God.***

1 Corinthians 2:10

For you to grasp the deep mysteries of God, you need the baptism in the Holy Spirit. Jesus said:

> *I have yet many things to say unto you, but ye cannot bear them now.*
>
> *Howbeit when he, the Spirit of truth, is come he*

108

will guide you into all truth....

John 16:12-13

If you want to go all the length in the knowledge of God's will for you, you need the baptism in the Holy Spirit.

Lastly, you should be involved in the fellowship of His children. We are told not to forsake the assembly of one another. It is during our gathering together that we "*...give attention to: reading, to exhortation, to doctrine...*" (1 Tim. 4:13).

The sharing of God's mysteries, in accordance with what each of His children has received, benefits the whole body. At such times, the operations of the gifts of the Holy Spirit are most active. Prophecies and other revelation gifts shed more light on His will, consoling, advising, exhorting and exposing the activities of the devil in the body. But if you stand alone, you expose yourself to danger.

Be in fellowship with God's precious people. It is there that God commands the blessing (Psa. 133:1-3).

Understand that you do not know enough. The Bible says:

And if any man think that he knoweth any thing, he knoweth nothing yet as he ought to know.

1 Corinthians 8:2

You need others to teach and enlighten you. The diversities of the ministry gifts are not vested in one person; they are shared in the body. What you have cannot meet all your spiritual needs. Therefore, wherever you are, look out for a Holy Ghost fellowship and be part of what God is doing there. This is very important. Clear off from bad company, and create a conducive atmosphere for productive meditation.

This act of meditation will produce faith in you. If you meditate on healing scriptures, you will be able to release your faith in that area. If it is in provision, the fact that the word has gained entrance into you by the Holy Ghost puts you on to be able to release your faith in that direction. You will need to release your faith to get your victory.

CHAPTER 9

PRESENT YOUR CASE

If you want money from your bank, two basic conditions must be met. A fully-signed cheque in your hand, and an amount of money in the account commensurate with the amount stated on the cheque. If these two conditions are satisfied, you go to the bank, present your cheque, and wait until your money is delivered to you. Several people may be at the bank waiting to withdraw money, but hardly does a situation arise whereby one customer's money is given to the other.

In the presentation of your request as a believer,

this is, in a way, the procedure you adopt. There is an account in heaven for you. Whether you are aware of such fact or not makes no difference; it is there. It is an account overflowing with the riches of God in Christ Jesus. The riches are inexhaustible, and the variety unlimited. But they are made available upon request. The Word says, *"he that asketh receiveth."* This is a foremost rule to bear in mind. It is not he that believes that receives, but he that believes and translates his belief into action by asking. Remember, it is not faith that heals the sick, but the prayer of faith.

> *...The prayer of faith shall save the sick ...*
>
> James 5:15

Therefore, it is belief or faith followed by asking that establishes the promise for you. Your prayer must first remind God of His promises concerning that need, because He demands that you:

> *Put me in remembrance: let us plead together: declare thou, that thou mayest be justified.*
>
> Isaiah 43:26

Then you give your tangible reasons for your request, because, again, God says:

> *Produce your cause, saith the LORD; bring forth your strong reasons, saith the King of Jacob.*
>
> Isaiah 41:21

112

Your prayer is not telling God what is happening. He knows it already. It is telling Him what you want Him to do for you, by reminding Him of His word concerning your situation. If you are troubled by sickness for instance, you have a case. The Word has made provisions for your healing. The Bible says healing is children's bread. It is also written:

> *Surely he hath borne our griefs (sickness), and carried our sorrows (pains)... and with his stripes we are healed.*
>
> Isaiah 53:4-5

If you are a child of God, then healing is your entitlement. So set out to present your case, and God will surely justify you. There is no way He can deny Himself. He is keeping watch over His word to perform it.

Remember, God does not need any healing; there is no sickness up there in heaven. It is you who needs healing, money, fertile womb, etc. Go ahead, therefore, to present your case to Him in firm assurance that whatever you ask, you will receive from Him. That is a benefit of your sonship.

CHAPTER 10

ADDRESS THE SITUATION

You have put God in remembrance, you have given Him your strong reasons. Faith has now sprung up in your heart. You now have boldness from the assurance of God's approval and presence. Now, you turn and face the odds that have been harassing you. You speak out the way you want things to be, and your decree will be established in heaven.

You have to do the addressing yourself, because God is not going to do it for you. When Jesus Christ was at Lazarus' tomb, He did not ask God to speak to the dead man. Jesus did it Himself. He addressed the dead body, *"Lazarus come forth."* He told His disciples:

> *...Whosoever shall say unto this mountain, Be thou removed, and be thou cast into the sea; and shall not doubt in his heart, but shall believe that those things which he saith shall come to pass; he shall have whatsoever he saith.*
>
> Mark 11:23

In the case concerning the welfare of my son, I went straight to address the situation. I said, "Boy, I prophesy to you: you shall eat and shall not vomit, you shall sleep, and your sleep shall be sweet." That settled it. He ate, and for the first time in three days, he did not vomit. And what's more, he went into a very deep sleep. Praise the Lord! Jesus is real. The Bible says, *"The strangers shall hear my voice, and as soon as they do they shall fade away from their hiding places"* (Psalm 18:44-45).

It is very important here for you to note that there is great power in your mouth. There is a deposit of creative power in you. The moment you get what the word says about your situation, and faith is built up, you present your case, and then stand to address the situation, the creative miraculous power is released into the situation. By this you have mobilized the host of heaven into swift action, and they handle the situation with dispatch. But the word of the miraculous has to be released from your mouth before this can be done.

> *But what saith it? The word is nigh thee, even in thy mouth, and in thy heart: that is, the word of faith, which we preach.*
>
> Romans 10:8

This word conceived in your heart, formed by the tongue, and spoke out of the mouth becomes a creative power that will work for you. If you take the word of God and speak it boldly to your situation by faith, it is as powerful and as effective as Jesus speaking it.

Once your word has gone forth in faith, forget about the imposing presence of the problem, or the horde of opposition that will hurl themselves against you. The Word, which is sharper than any two-edged sword, has gone to the root of the problem. What remains is like a huge superstructure without a base – its collapse is only a matter of time.

When Jesus Christ cursed the fruitless fig tree, there was no immediate outward manifestation of the effect of the curse. Nevertheless, in the spirit realm, where the vital forces controlling life lie, the tree had ceased to exist. Therefore, any appearance of your mountain, any impression of things getting worse even after you have addressed the mountain is a sign of victory.

The devils Jesus cast out rent their victims sore before departing. When a snake's head is cut off, the body writhes and convulses. That is exactly what happens when you address your "mountain." Do not shift your ground after you have addressed the situation. See it as done.

CHAPTER II

DECLARE YOUR VICTORY

Victory is not only demonstrated in action, but in words also. When you are relaxed over victory, your confidence will definitely find expression in your language. You talk positive things. Your optimism brings out utterances like, "It is done", or "I have received." There are no "ifs." The things you are looking forward to receiving have become so real to you that you are completely absorbed in calculating the details.

Your utterances bewilder the unbeliever, because of, perhaps, the formidable nature of the odds against you. He asks you, "Are you so sure this will be possible?" Your confident answer can only add to his confusion.

He may even entertain some doubt about your mental state. Could you be such a dolt (stupid fellow) as to count your chickens before they are hatched? But that is precisely how you are to appear before the world, if you really want your victory. You must observe all the rules, because half measures carry no weight in the spirit realm. It is written:

...whosoever shall keep the whole law, and yet offend in one point, he is guilty of all.

James 2:10

This is as true of the law handed down to the Israelites, as it is of the other rules or laws of the spirit that lead to victory in life.

You have got to proclaim your victory, because the light (faith) in your heart must be known to the world outside. The Bible says, *"No man lighteth a lamp and hideth it under a bushel."* When you set the lamp on a table, all darkness is driven away. When you proclaim your victory, you put all demonic hosts to flight, because they simply cannot stand faith-loaded utterances. It bewilders them.

Jesus emphasized the importance of the words you speak out. He said:

For by thy words thou shalt be justified, and by thy

power of tongue (decrees)

words thou shalt be condemned.

Matthew 12:37

That is a basic truth of life since the creation of man. The people of Israel literally talked themselves out of their possession of the promised land at Kadesh Barnea. They confessed and declared their inability. They said, "We cannot go in. The people are stronger and mightier. There is no way we can win." God also told them:

As truly as I live… as ye have spoken in mine ears, so will I do to you.

Numbers 14:28

40 yrs of deliverance

They talked themselves out of it and had to spend extra 40 years to get into it. Wrong confession will cost you your victory. It may even cost you money and if you are not careful, it will cost you your life.

"Death and life are in the power of the tongue" (Prov. 14:28), because the tongue is the outlet for the abundance contained in the heart of man.

Note that what you are now is a product of what you have said about yourself in the past. Jesus said there is no way a spring can bring forth both sweet and bitter water. You cannot say one thing and expect a different thing to happen. That is not possible. What proceeds from your mouth is a spiritual force that makes or unmakes you.

If your heart has negative ideas, your words will definitely be negative. And negative words will yield failure and frustration. On the other hand, a heart full of healthy, holy ideas shall yield success, joy and life abundant. The Psalmist says:

> *What man is he that desireth life, and loveth many days, that he may see good?*
>
> *Keep thy tongue from evil, and thy lips from speaking guile.*
>
> Psalm 34:12-13

But if you want to speak the right words, you have to load yourself with the word of His grace, and your words will give grace to all your hearers and bring your victories home.

CHAPTER 12

DEMONSTRATE YOUR VICTORY

I have said that believing the promises of God does not guarantee you answers, except you translate your belief into action. That is faith in action, or faith backed by works.

When you address your situation, you go into action regardless of your feelings or appearances to the contrary. This is your demonstration of victory. It is a walk into victory, confirming the finality of what you have spoken. If your action is actually springing from genuine faith, obstacles will crumble, revealing those needs which are as eagerly looking for you as you are for them.

The demonstration of victory is important because

God does not judge by mere lip confession, but by life expressions. The Bible says:

> *...**For the LORD is a God of knowledge, and by him actions are weighed.***

1 Samuel 2:3

That is to say, He justifies you on the basis of what proceeds out of your heart.

> *I the LORD search the heart, I try the reins, even to give every man according to his ways, and according to the fruit of his doings.*

Jeremiah 17:10

Your actions are controlled by the state of your heart. The Bible says "...*out of the heart are the issues of life.*" Jesus also emphasized the same point to His disciples in Matthew chapter 15.

Your actions must agree with your words. You cannot say, *"by his stripes I was healed"* and continue to patronize the chemist's shops, looking for Panadol. You are saying one thing and doing another. That is not confession. Nothing is going to work for you. Your actions must correspond with your declarations. James spoke about your actions confirming your faith. That is, faith and corresponding action. Be sure to take time to do what you say.

124

The Bible records instances of classic demonstration of victory that changed the destinies of the persons concerned. Hannah, who later became the mother of Samuel, was one of such persons. The Bible records that when she had finished supplicating for a child from the Lord, she did not continue to wear her previous mournful look, but, *"she went her way, and did eat and her countenance was no more sad"* (1 Sam. 1:18).

David was another person who believed in action after confession. He believed God was able to deliver Goliath into his hand, so he went straight into action. There was not a single soldier in the ranks of Israel's army who could claim to believe that God could defeat the hosts of the Philistine. Their action was enough proof that they did not believe God for victory.

Anxiety and fear are enemies of faith. They manifest themselves in actions. Anxiety breeds fear, and fear breeds doubt, which will rob you of every promise of the word.

Fret not thyself ...

Psalm 37:1

> *Be careful for nothing...*
>
> Philippians 4:6

Anxiety and fear are spiritual forces. They seek to entangle you in your Christian walk, to draw you into the sense realm, and render you unsuitable to fight your spiritual battles. But you can resist them. The Bible says:

> *For God hath not given us the spirit of fear; but of power, and of love, and of a sound mind.*
>
> 2 Timothy 1:7

Moreover, you are to *"resist the devil and he will flee from you."* Whatever tree your heavenly Father has not planted, you can uproot. You do not uproot the tree by fretting, because by that you will only succeed in uprooting your own self.

> *Which of you by taking thought can add one cubit unto his stature?*
>
> Matthew 6:27

Yes, your fretting and doubting will harm you physically and prevent you from receiving from the Lord. Be good to yourself. Be relaxed and comfortable. Let your actions reveal that your heart is fixed, trusting the Lord. You have addressed the mountain, now go through as if it has disappeared and it will flee from your presence. As the Israelites moved towards the Red sea, the Bible says:

The sea saw it (their faith in action), and fled...

Psalm 114:3

Halleluyah!

CHAPTER 13

REFUSE TO QUIT

The last step to your victory is to refuse to quit. You have got God's word about the situation, you have built up your faith in that direction, you have presented your case, and you have addressed the situation. You have also declared your victory and are now demonstrating it. Your victory is already certain. It has now been released in the heavenlies. The angels – your ministering spirits - are working hard on its manifestation. You are at the point of having it. So do not quit.

Jesus said:

...What things soever ye desire, when ye pray, believe that ye receive them, and ye shall have them.

Mark 11:24

There is a period between receiving and having it. This is the period that your sincerity about the other six steps will be tested.

Do you really believe what you are doing? Do you expect any result from your actions? This is the time you will prove it. Stand there and refuse to quit. One thing is sure, the result will come. It is not possible for anything to stop it from coming. Nothing can stand against your victory. You are the most important factor in this area. You cannot quit, if you really have faith in what you are doing. A winner does not quit, and a quitter does not, and cannot win. It is a spiritual law. Stand firmly. Refuse to shift your ground. If you do this, your victory is certain.

Abraham is a classic example here. He did not consider the situations around him. He kept standing on what God had told him. He was in the best position to doubt and quit, but he knew that if God's word was to work for him, he had to stick with it, so he did not quit.

He staggered not at the promise of God through unbelief; but was strong in faith, giving glory to God;

And being fully persuaded that, what he had promised, he was able also to perform.

Romans 4:20-21

He had a choice to be strong in faith or to be weak in faith. He had a choice to stagger or not to stagger. All the options were open to him, but he refused to quit. He was fully persuaded about God's ability to fulfill His promise.

God met Abraham because he refused to quit. You will also need to be fully persuaded. Know enough of God to stand on His word and refuse to quit. Remember, a winner does not quit, and a quitter does not, and cannot win.

ACKNOWLEDGE THE RECEIPT

God requires and deserves your art and act of acknowledgement. One reason people have been shut-off from the blessings of the Lord is their lack of acknowledgement. Every believer must be quick to express the fact that it is not by power nor by might, but by the Spirit of the Lord that his victory has come. It is God at work to do His own pleasure in you. The Psalmist always took time to acknowledge the wondrous deeds of the Lord.

Bless the LORD, O my soul, and forget not all his benefits:

> *Who forgiveth all thine iniquities; who healeth all thy diseases;*
>
> *Who redeemeth thy life from destruction; who crowneth thee with lovingkindness and tender mercies.*
>
> Psalm 103:2-4

He knew he needed to bless the Lord for these benefits of forgiveness, healing and redemption. He knew this would endear him to God's heart, and move Him to do more for him. You also need to give thanks to God after you have done all these.

You do not necessarily need to see the victory before you begin to acknowledge the receipt. As you give thanks to the Lord, He is impressed about your faith. It is then that you are really walking in faith. Your principle is not "seeing is believing", but "believing is seeing." Believing actions of praise and giving of thanks endear you to God's heart and enhances your confidence in the release of your victory.

> *In every thing give thanks: for this is the will of God in Christ Jesus concerning you.*
>
> 1 Thessalonians 5:18

God is interested in you giving Him thanks. You have to be quick to acknowledge God's goodness in your life, and do it constantly.

The Lord Jesus demonstrated and emphasized the need and importance of giving of thanks. He was passing through Samaria to Jerusalem one day and there were ten lepers outside the city. They shouted to Him with a loud voice for help. He then instructed them to go and show themselves to the priests. As they went, they were healed, and one of them came back to testify and acknowledge his healing.

> *And one of them, when he saw that he was healed, turned back, and with a loud voice glorified God,*
>
> *And fell down on his face at his feet, giving him thanks: and he was a Samaritan.*
>
> *And Jesus answering said, Were there not ten cleansed? but where are the nine?*
>
> *There are not found that returned to give glory to God, save this stranger.*
>
> Luke 17:15-18

It is obvious here that it is important for you to give glory to God for the receipt of your victory. In everything, give thanks to God. The act of ingratitude to God is sinful and attracts curses from the Lord.

> *If ye will not hear, and if ye will not lay it to heart, to give glory unto my name, saith the LORD of hosts, I will even send a curse upon you, and I will curse your blessings: yea, I have cursed them*

135

already, because ye do not lay it to heart.

Malachi 2:2

It is that serious. God deserves and requires your thanksgiving. Take time to give glory to His name. He is worthy to be praised. He has been wonderful and good to you. You have a duty to give praise and thanks to His name. Many people neglect this and they run into unnecessary difficulties in life. They began to pray and fast, not knowing that they are responsible for their woes, simply because they do not lay it to heart to give glory to God.

He will not share His glory with any man. He is supreme and mighty. In fact, there are many reasons why you need to give God thanks. Look at things around you, and you will discover that the race is not to the swift.

...It is not of him that willeth, nor of him that runneth, but of God that sheweth mercy.

Romans 9:16

...The race is not to the swift, nor the battle to the strong, neither yet bread to the wise, nor yet riches to men of understanding, nor yet favour to men of skill....

Ecclesiastes 9:11

It is absolutely the mercy and the doing of the Lord.

136

Paul said, *"By the grace of God I am what I am..."* (1 Corinthians 15:10).

Whatever victory you win is by His grace. By the finished work of Christ you got it; not by your strength.

It is very important, therefore, that you lay it to heart to bless and give glory to God in all things. It will also help your faith a lot. You will have confidence to go before God always for another round of victory, if you take time to acknowledge the previous ones.

> *That the communication of the faith may become effectual by thy acknowledging of every good thing which is in you by Christ Jesus.*
>
> Philemon 6

Acknowledge those good things (your victories) in your life, and your faith will be more effectually communicated.

You are born a winner!

ABOUT THE AUTHOR

For more than two decades, Dr. David O. Oyedepo, has been part of the current charismatic renaissance sweeping through the African continent. His faith-based teachings have transformed millions of lives.

Called with a specific mandate to liberate mankind from all oppressions of the devil, Dr. Oyedepo is the President of Living Faith Church Worldwide Inc., with a network of churches all over Nigeria and most nations of Africa.

He is also the Senior Pastor of the 50,000 capacity - Faith Tabernacle, Canaan Land, Ota, a suburb of Lagos, Nigeria reputed to be the largest church auditorium in the world.

As an educationist, his mission currently pioneers the establishment of educational institutions at all levels in Nigeria, including the recently established Covenant University, where he serves as the Chancellor.

He has written over 50 titles of inspirational and educative texts covering various aspects of life.

He is married to Faith, and their marriage is blessed with children.

Books By Dr. David Oyedepo

- In Pursuit Of Vision
- Pillars Of Destiny
- Signs & Wonders Today
- Exploits In Ministry
- Winning The War Against Poverty
- Walking In Dominion
- Possessing Your Possession
- The Wisdom That Works
- Exploits Of Faith
- Anointing For Exploits
- Understanding The Power Of Praise
- Walking In Newness Of Life
- Maximise Destiny
- Commanding The Supernatural
- Winning Invisible Battles
- Success Systems
- Understanding Financial Prosperity
- Success Strategies
- Understanding Your Covenant Right
- Exploring the Riches of Redemption
- Anointing For Breakthrough
- Excellency Of Wisdom
- Breaking Financial Hardship
- The Release Of Power
- Walking In The Miraculous
- Satan Get Lost!
- The Winning Wisdom
- Walking In Wisdom
- The Healing Balm

INSIDE VIEW OF
Faith Tabernacle
OUTSIDE VIEW OF FAITH TABERNACLE
CHURCH MASS TRANSIT— Over 250 buses commuting the worshippers to Church from all nook and crannies of Lagos & environs
Dr. David Oyedepo is the founding president of the Living Faith Church Worldwide Inc. And senior pastor of the Faith Tabernacle, a 50,000 capacity sanctuary located in Canaan Land, Ota, a suburb of Lagos Nigeria.
The construction of this gigantic architectural masterpiece was completed within twelve months and dedicated on September 18, 1999. Built totally debt free and without any foreign inputs! To God alone be all the glory.
Today, Faith Tabernacle stands as the home of signs and wonders for men and women all over the world who keep coming in droves to worship the King of kings and Lord of lords, Jesus Christ the Son of the Living God.
Visit our website for more information: www.davidoyedepoministries.org

Covenant University

Dr. David Oyedepo is the visioner and Chancellor of Covenant University founded 21st October 2002. Today, Covenant University has student population of over 6,000, all fully boarded on campus; in a state of the art halls of residence. All degree programmes offered at Covenant University are fully accredited by the appropriate accrediting body. As at date, CU offers 42 degree programmes in 3 different faculties:

COLLEGE OF SCIENCE AND TECHNOLOGY:

Computer Science, Management Information System, Architecture, Building Technology, Estate Management, Industrial Mathematics, Industrial Chemistry, Industrial Physics, Biochemistry, Biology, Microbiology, Computer Engineering, Information and Communication Technology, Electrical and Electronic Engineering, Civil Engineering, Mechanical Engineering, Chemical Engineering, Petroleum Engineering.

COLLEGE OF HUMAN DEVELOPMENT:

Philosophy, Psychology, Counseling, English Language, Mass Communication, Public Relations and Advertising, Sociology and French.

COLLEGE OF BUSINESS AND SOCIAL SCIENCES:

Accounting, Taxation and Public Sector Accounting, Banking and Finance, Business Administration, Marketing, Industrial Relations and Human Resource Management, Economics, Demography and Social Statistics, International Relations, Political Science, Public Administration, Policy and Strategic Studies.

More Facilities@ Covenant University

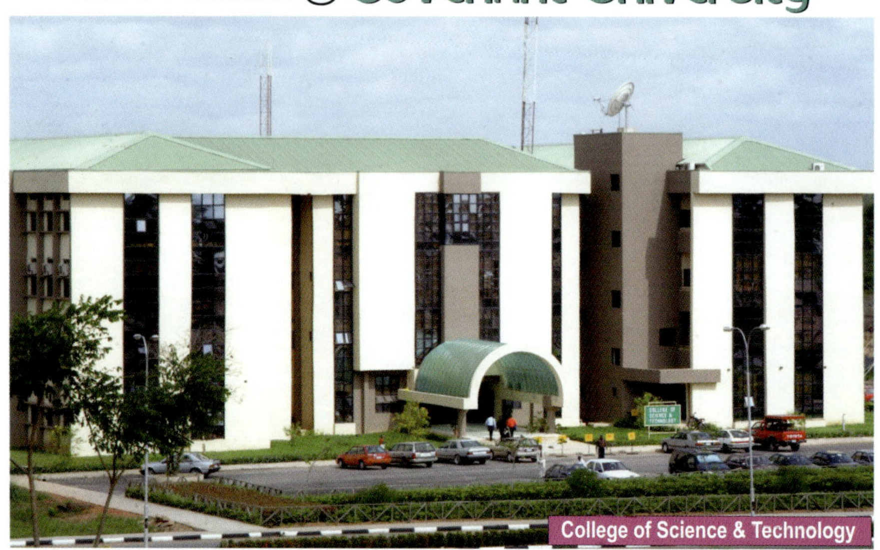

College of Science & Technology

University Library (Centre For Learning Resources)

4,000 Seat Students Chapel